World of Islam

Divisions Within Islam

MASON CREST PUBLISHERS
PHILADELPHIA

World of Islam

World of Islam

Divisions Within Islam

JOHN CALVERT

Editorial Consultants: Foreign Policy Research Institute, Philadelphia, PA

Mason Crest Publishers
370 Reed Road
Broomall, PA 19008
www.masoncrest.com

First printing

1 3 5 7 9 8 6 4 2

Library of Congress Cataloging-in-Publication Data

Calvert, John.
  Divisions in Islam / John Calvert.
     p. cm.
  ISBN 978-1-4222-0533-4 (hardcover) — ISBN 978-1-4222-0804-5 (pbk.)
  1. Islamic sects—Juvenile literature. I. Title.
  BP191.C35 2009
  297.8—dc22
                              2009019999

Photo Credits: 7: Used under license from Shutterstock, Inc.; 9: Abdullah Y. Al-Dobrais/Saudi Aramco
World/Padia; 11: Used under license from Shutterstock, Inc.; 14: Used under license from Shutterstock, Inc.;
15: Michael Di Biase/Saudi Aramco World/Padia; 16: Used under license from Shutterstock, Inc.; 18: Used under
license from Shutterstock, Inc.; 20: U.S. Navy Photo by Photographer's Mate 1st Class Arlo K. Abrahamson/DoD;
23: U.S. Army Photo by Spc. Luke Thornberry/DoD; 24: U.S. Air Force Photo by Staff Sgt. Manuel J. Martinez/DoD;
27: Katrina Thomas/Saudi Aramco World/Padia; 29: © istockphoto.com/syagci; 30: evilz_eagelz
(www.flickr.com/photos/85941387@N00/921509584); 32: Foundation of Holy Defence Values, Archives, and
Publications (www.sajed.ir); 34: Hussain A. Al-Ramadan/Saudi Aramco World/Padia; 35: © istockphoto.com/
onfilm; 38: © European Communities; 41: Used under license from Shutterstock, Inc.; 43: UN Photo;
46: Library of Congress; 49: Used under license from Shutterstock, Inc.; 53: Georges Jansoone (http://
commons.wikimedia.org/wiki/File:Turkey.Konya021.jpg); 54: Courtesy Turkish Tourist Office

John Calvert is the Fr. Henry W. Casper Associate Professor of History at Creighton University where he teaches courses
related to the medieval and modern periods of Islamic history. He has published widely on Islamist movements and thinkers
and is regularly interviewed by the media on current developments in the Middle East.

World of Islam

Table of Contents

Sunni Islam

It is the mark of a great world religion to accommodate different outlooks and sensibilities. Quite often, these differences are manifested in terms of formal divisions within the faith. Thus, in Christianity, a distinction exists between the Roman Catholic Church and the various Protestant denominations. Judaism divides into the Orthodox, Conservative, and Reform movements. The major division in Buddhism is between the Theravada and Mahayana forms of the faith.

Islam is no exception to this rule. In Islam, the major split is between Sunni and the various forms of Shiism, though other divisions also exist. This book will describe and explain these divisions, focusing on Shiism but also taking into consideration other important interpretations of Islam. In contrast to Christianity, the divisions of Islam tend to have their origins in politics rather than dogma. Although theological questions do form part of these divisions, the issues over which they first crystallized were primarily concerned with the leadership of the Islamic community (*umma*).

Pilgrims process around the Kaaba, an ancient shrine in Mecca, Saudi Arabia, that Muslims consider the holiest place in the world. Although there are many sects or divisions within Islam, all Muslims share certain fundamental beliefs, known as the Five Pillars of Islam.

It will be useful to begin with a few words about Sunni Islam, the position held by approximately 90 percent of the world's Muslims, from which the sectarian forms of Islam, with which we are concerned, are distinguished.

According to the majority Sunni view, the Prophet Muhammad died in 632 C.E. without naming a successor. If Muhammad had had a son, the Muslims at Medina might easily have settled the issue of the succession, but the one son born to the Prophet died in infancy. Thus, it was left to the community of Muslims at Medina to decide the matter. Some of the elders of the community gathered to decide how to hold the people together and ensure some form of continuity. After deliberating, the elders determined that one of Muhammad's closet companions, the venerable tribal *shaykh* ("elder") Abu Bakr, should be the caliph, or "successor" to the Prophet. In many ways, Abu Bakr was the logical choice. He was an early convert to Islam, he was an older man who knew the tribes and their genealogies, and his daughter Aisha had been one of Muhammad's wives.

Although it was clear to the Muslims that Muhammad was the last of the prophets, no one in the Muslim community was quite sure what the role of Abu Bakr should be. However, within a short time, a consensus emerged among the Muslims that the caliph's chief duties should be to enforce Qur'anic laws, defend Islam from its enemies, and expand the faith beyond the Arabian Peninsula, where Islam had originated. According to the Sunnis, the caliphs were mortals who did not have divine powers or even special insight. Their authority was limited to worldly affairs. Sunnis left matters of religious guidance in the hands of the *ulama*, religious scholars who specialized in the interpretation of the Qur'an and the specifics of its application in society. Early on, the Muslims at Medina decided that the caliphs should be elected or chosen from the tribe of Quraysh, Muhammad's tribe.

Abu Bakr ruled as caliph only two years. Before he died in 634, he appointed another early convert to Islam, Umar, to become the next caliph. A resentful servant attacked Umar in 644. Before he died, he appointed a committee, called a *shura*, to select the next caliph. The committee chose Uthman. In many ways, Uthman was an unlikely candidate. He hailed from a clan—the Umayyads—that had earlier resisted Muhammad and the Muslims. However, Uthman's piety distinguished him from his Umayyad kinsmen. It was he who had the Qur'an collected and put into an authorized version. Mutinous Muslim soldiers who had settled in Egypt murdered Uthman in 656. The community next chose as caliph Ali, the Prophet Muhammad's cousin and son-in-law (he was married to one of the Prophet's daughters, Fatima).

Each year, millions of Muslims visit the Prophet's Mosque in Medina, Saudi Arabia, which contains Muhammad's tomb. The tombs of the first two caliphs, Abu Bakr and Umar, are also located within the Prophet's Mosque.

Collectively, Sunni Muslims refer to Abu Bakr, Umar, Uthman, and Ali as the *Rashidun* ("rightly guided") caliphs, so called because each knew the Prophet Muhammad personally and dedicated himself to maintaining his ways. In the Sunni Muslim perspective, the short-lived era of the Rashidun represents the high point of Islam in history. Even today, Muslims regard the period as exemplary. Of course, modern Muslims have no interest in replicating the primitive material culture of the Rashidun era. Yet many recognize that these early caliphs implemented Qur'anic principles in society to a degree that subsequent Muslim rulers did not match. Although the dynasties of caliphs that followed the Rashidun—the Umayyads (ruled 661–750) and the Abbasids (ruled 750–1258)—built up Islam's power and prestige in the world, they do not have quite the same reputation in Sunni Muslim eyes. Sunni Muslims accuse a number of these caliphs of indiscretions and bad behavior.

Nevertheless, Sunni Muslims recognize the legitimacy not only of the Rashidun but also of all the caliphs, including those of the Umayyad and Abbasid dynasties. The strength of the Sunni position rests in the belief that it is preferable to accept a ruler who is less than ideal than to risk strife and factionalism. In fact, at most times in history the Sunni establishment has adopted a very comprehensive attitude and tried to include as many Muslims as it could under the Sunni umbrella—even when this meant that the notion of acceptable Sunni belief had to adapt and expand. In the traditional Sunni view, one can disagree with the way rulers govern Muslim countries, yet it is always better to preserve the integrity of the Muslim community than risk civil war.

The very term *Sunni*, the name Sunnis use to refer to themselves, reflects the ideal of community solidarity: "the people of tradition (*sunna*) and the community." Historically, Sunni

The third caliph, Uthman ibn Affan, ruled the Muslim community from 644 to 656. During his rule, Uthman directed the creation of a standard written version of the Qur'an, the sacred scripture of Islam. Muslims believe that the Qur'an contains Allah's laws and directions for humanity, which were given to Muhammad between 610 and 632 C.E. The revelations were immediately memorized by Muhammad and his followers but were not compiled until the Caliphate of Uthman.

Muslims have looked to the consensus of the community, known as *ijma*, to determine points of doctrine and behavior. According to a well-known *hadith*, the Prophet Muhammad declared, "My people will never agree together on an error." Consensus therefore became a powerful force for conformity within Sunni Islam.

By the early Middle Ages, various schools of law had developed among Sunni Muslims. These were the Hanafi, Shafii, Maliki, and Hanbali schools of jurisprudence. Although these schools differed slightly in terms of the methodology they employed to discover God's will, all agreed on the Qur'an and the example of the Prophet Muhammad as the ultimate sources of truth.

The Kharijites

Uthman's murder precipitated Islam's first civil war, which in turn led to the first division within Muslim ranks. After Uthman's death, most of the Muslims proclaimed Ali as the next caliph. Although Ali assumed the position of caliph, he did not bring Uthman's murderers to justice. Ali's refusal to take action angered Uthman's kinsman Mu'awiyya. Mu'awiyya, governor of Damascus, was leader of the Umayyad clan following Uthman's death. He demanded that Ali hand the murderers over to him for punishment, so that justice might be done in accordance with the laws of the Qur'an. The issue eventually came to a head. Both Mu'awiyya and Ali gathered together armies, which met in 657 near Siffin on the Euphrates River.

After several months of inconclusive skirmishing, men from Mu'awiyya's army approached Ali's camp with Qur'ans raised on their spears. They said that it was not right that Muslims should fight one another, and they called for arbitration. Ali took up the offer, and representatives from the two sides discussed their differences. The negotiations resulted in deadlock, but not before tribesmen from Ali's camp abandoned the field, claiming that Ali and Mu'awiyya had sinned by subjecting the matter between them to human, as opposed to divine, judgment. In their view, there was "no judgment except that of God." Only God, through the Qur'an, had made binding laws for humankind; Ali and Mu'awiyya did not sufficiently reference the divine judgment in their deliberations, and thus had usurped the divine prerogative.

These rebellious tribesmen were called "Kharijites"—literally, "those who secede" or "go out," referring to their sudden exit from Ali's army. They held a strict, activist position. In their view, all who fell short of total adherence to the teachings in the Qur'an were disbelievers who must be resisted. In the eyes of the Kharijites, Muslims had a sacred duty to call a caliph, or other Muslim, to account for his errors. If the offending Muslim repented, they recognized him as a member of the "true" community of believers. If he failed to respond properly, then they were to target him through jihad (holy war waged on behalf of Islam).

In fact, in 661, four years after their departure from the field at Siffin, the Kharijites murdered the caliph Ali as he prayed at the mosque at Najaf, in what is today Iraq. In their opinion, he had shown no remorse over his actions at Siffin, and therefore was deserving of death. Mu'awiyya, Ali's erstwhile enemy, then became caliph and founder of the Umayyad dynasty. Largely in response to the uncompromising outlook of the Kharijites, the Sunnis developed their inclusive understanding of who was a Muslim. According to Sunni theology, if a person confessed Islam—even while acting badly—then the community must accept that person as a legitimate Muslim.

Unlike the Sunnis who restricted the caliphs to Muhammad's tribe of Quraysh, and the Shia who traced the line of Muslim leaders though Ali and his descendants, the Kharijites did not place conditions regarding birth. The Kharijites maintained that

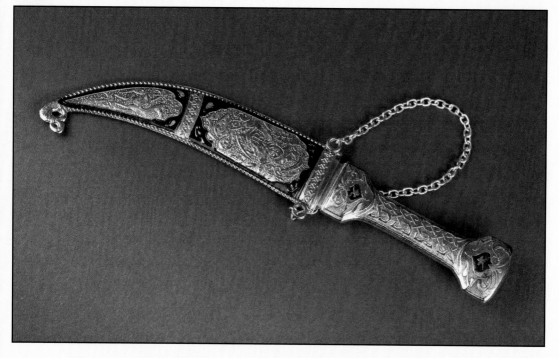

Today many Muslims view the time of the "rightly guided" caliphs as a golden age of Islam. However, during this time the Muslim community was torn by violent disputes over leadership.

any Kharijite Muslim could become caliph as long as he was of sound character. Before the Kharijites, Muslims reserved the term *kafir* ("disbeliever") for individuals outside of the Islamic community. The Kharijites called disbelievers those who claimed to be Muslim but did not live up to the religious standards that they had set. They thus made a distinction between true Muslims, who were Kharijites, and false Muslims, who rejected Kharijite Islam. Consciously imitating Muhammad's flight (*hijra*) from Mecca to Medina, Kharijite groups fled to the desert where they made war on other Muslims, whom they viewed as infidels. However, Kharijite successes were few. Although they gained some support among the Bedouins and peasants, with one or two exceptions they rarely took control of cities or established a powerful state of their own.

The Sunni caliphs suppressed most of the Kharijite groups in the course of the early medieval period. In response to these defeats, a Kharijite leader named Abdullah ibn Ibad developed in 684 a version of Kharijite doctrine that allowed Kharijites to live, at least temporarily, with the reality of "infidel" rule. Whereas the Kharijites had originally branded Muslims who committed offenses disbelievers meriting capital punishment, the Ibadis saw such people as monotheists who were ungrateful for the blessings God had granted them. The Ibadi attitude toward such people, whether they be sinning Ibadis or non-Ibadi Muslims, was that one should "dissociate" from them. It was not necessary to display toward them overt hostility. In common with original Kharijite teaching, the Ibadis chose their Imam for his knowledge and piety, without any regard to race or lineage, and were obligated to depose him if he acted unjustly.

The Ibadis created a prosperous state, based at the city of Tahert, among the Berber people of western Algeria. However, in the 10th century the state was destroyed by the rival Fatimid power based in Egypt. Surviving Ibadi communities in North Africa exist in the Mzab Valley of Saharan Algeria, in the Nafus mountains of Libya, and on the island of Jerba in Tunisia. Another relatively powerful Ibadi state took root in Oman in the Arabian Peninsula, where Ibadism continues as the official creed of the country.

This gold coin, issued by the Umayyad caliph Abd al-Malik, was struck at the Damascus mint around 693 C.E. The Umayyad dynasty of Islamic rulers was established by Mu'awiyya after the assassination of Ali in 661.

Night falls over the Grand Mosque of Oman. Most people in this sultanate on the coast of the Arabian Peninsula are Ibadi Muslims.

Beginning in the 1960s, many Sunni ulama applied the term Kharijite to a number of the radical Islamist groups that had emerged in Egypt and elsewhere in the Middle East. The term appeared appropriate to these scholars: Like the Kharijites of old, the radical Islamists called into question the faith of Muslim rulers whose rule appeared to them not to be Islamic. Of course, the radicals were not truly Kharijites: they operated according to their own set of beliefs, which they derived from the Qur'an, erroneously in the view of most Muslims.

3

Twelver Shiism

Shiism is the second-largest denomination of Islam, after Sunni Islam. Today, the Shia comprise about 10 percent of the total population of Muslims in the world. The most important group within the Shia is the "Twelvers," so called for the 12 Imams, or leaders, they venerate. The largest concentrations of Shia Muslims are found in the Islamic Republic of Iran, where they make up 89 percent of the country's total population; Iraq, where they comprise 63 percent of the country's total; and Lebanon, where they are 41 percent of the total population. Numerically significant Twelver Shia communities also exist in the Arab Gulf (Bahrain, Kuwait, and northeastern Saudi Arabia), Afghanistan, Pakistan, and India. Subgroups within the Shia include the Zaydis, who exist mostly in Yemen; and the Ismailis, who live mainly in India, in East Africa, and in scattered communities in North America and Western Europe. Most of what follows applies to the Twelver Shia, although in following chapters we will also say something about the Zaydis and the Ismailis.

Shia Muslims participate in the Friday community prayer at a mosque in Isfahan, Iran. Shiites make up about 10 percent of the total Muslim population worldwide. Iran is one of the few countries where they constitute a majority.

In terms of beliefs and religious practices, Sunnis and Shia have much in common. Both communities believe in God (Allah) and his prophet Muhammad; each regards the Qur'an as the exact word of God; and each upholds the obligations to pray, fast, dispense charity, and perform the hajj at Mecca. Where the two branches differ is over the question of who should hold the political leadership (*Imamate*) of the Islamic community. The Sunnis believe that the Prophet Muhammad died without saying anything about who should take his place as leader of the Muslims. Therefore, the Muslims at Medina took the initiative and chose from their ranks the Rashidun caliphs. Following the Rashidun, the Ummayad and Abbasid caliphs provided the Sunni Muslims with leadership.

In contrast to the Sunnis, the Shia believe that Muhammad did in fact name a successor: Ali ibn Abi Talib. According to

Shia tradition, a few weeks before his death, at a place called Ghadir Khumm, Muhammad took Ali by the hand, raised it, and proclaimed before the Muslims who were assembled there, "Everyone whose patron I am, also has Ali as patron. O Allah, befriend every friend of Ali and be the enemy of all his enemies; help those that aid him and abandon all who desert him." On the same occasion, the Shia believe, Muhammad underlined his trust in Ali in uttering these words: "I leave behind you two things which, if you cleave to them, you will never go astray— that is, the Book of Allah and my offspring from my family [Ahl al-Bayt]."

For the Shia, Muhammad's statements at Ghadir Khumm confirm his—and God's—trust in Ali. Muhammad's affection and support for Ali were evident from the beginning. Ali was both Muhammad's cousin and his son-in-law—he was married to Muhammad's daughter Fatima. Having no surviving male heir, Muhammad loved Ali's sons, Hasan and Husayn. Moreover, Ali had been the first male to believe in Muhammad and the divine message that he preached. In the Shia view, these distinctions pointed to Ali's position as legitimate heir to Muhammad.

However, Ali was at first prevented from assuming the Imamate. As discussed in the previous chapter, other Companions of the Prophet—Abu Bakr, Umar, and Uthman—assumed the Imamate instead. Only in 656 did the Muslims at Medina elect Ali as community leader. In the Shia view, this is a position that he should have held upon the death of Muhammad. Almost immediately, Mu'awiyya, the Muslim governor of Syria, challenged Ali. The brief civil war between the two produced no clear victor. However, Ali's murder in 661 at the hands of a dissident group called the Kharijites (see previous chapter) cleared the way for Mu'awiyya to secure his claim to the caliphate. Mu'awiyya made sure that his son, Yazid, succeeded him. The dynasty that Mu'awiyya founded is the Umayyads, named after the clan within the Quraysh tribe to which he belonged.

Those who expressed a special loyalty or devotion to Ali took the title *Shiat Ali*, "the party (or faction) of Ali." From this phrase comes the simpler name, Shia. Gradually, over a period of three or four centuries, the Shia formed a distinct group, or sect, within Islam. Specifically, Shia doctrine holds that not only Ali, but all of the descendants of the Prophet Muhammad through the

This shrine to Ali ibn Abi Talib is located in the city of Najaf, in modern-day Iraq. Shiite Muslims believe that Ali, the cousin and son-in-law of Muhammad, was the rightful successor to the Prophet. They revere Ali's descendants as Imams—leaders of the Shiite community whom Allah intended to rule all Muslims.

line of Ali and Fatima, were most qualified to hold supreme political and religious authority over the Islamic community. Each descendant named the person within the family lineage who should succeed him. The Shia refer to these descendants of the Prophet as Imams (not to be confused with the prayer leader of a mosque, who is also called an imam). According to the Shia, the Sunni caliphs, including the Rashidun, Umayyads, and Abbasids, were usurpers who took over the leadership of the Islamic community by means of force and cunning. The authority of the Sunni caliphs, in the Shia view, is illegitimate.

For the Shia, the Imam is the inheritor of the teachings of the Prophet Muhammad. Imams thus have a special religious role that the Sunni caliphs did not possess. According to the Shia, God granted Muhammad special wisdom, which he transmitted to Ali, the first Imam. This wisdom then passed to the other descendants of Ali and Fatima. The Imams are not prophets. Both Shia and Sunnis agree that prophecy ended with the death of Muhammad. However, in the Shia view, the Imams are infallible. Because God preserves them from sin and error, their judgment on religious and worldly affairs is perfect. They can understand the hidden meanings of the Qur'an. Moreover, their insight allows them to interpret scripture in ways that take into consideration the changing circumstances of daily life. In some ways, the Shia Imams fulfill the role of community consensus in the Sunni tradition. Whereas in Sunni Islam, religious understanding emerges from the common agreement of the Islamic community, particularly the religious scholars (ulama), in Shiism understanding comes from the expert guidance of the Imams.

One of the key statements in the Qur'an around which much of the understanding on this issue rests is the verse "O believers! Obey God and obey the Apostle and those who have been given authority among you" (Qur'an 4:59). For Sunnis, "those who have been given authority" are the rulers (caliphs and sultans), but for the Shia this expression refers to the Imams.

The Imams provided religious guidance to their followers and contributed to the development of Shia thought. For example, the sixth Imam, Ja'far al-Sadiq (705–765), formulated the basic principles of Shia law. However, with the exception of Ali, the Sunni caliphs—Umayyad and Abbasid—never allowed the Imams to assume their roles as religious and political leaders of the Muslim community. The Sunni authorities persecuted and harassed the Imams and their followers. The Abbasid caliph Harun al-Rashid had the seventh Imam, Musa al-Kazim, killed. The Shia doctrine of *taqiyya* ("religious dissimulation"), by which the Shia considered it acceptable to conceal one's true allegiance in the face of adversity, derived from this situation of persecution.

The Shia hold Ali's second son, Husayn, whom they count as the third Imam, in high regard. During the first year of the caliph Yazid's reign, men who had supported Husayn's murdered father persuaded him to challenge the authority of the new Umayyad caliph. Husayn complied with the request and left Mecca with a force of 72 fighting men and their families. His destination was the city of Kufa in Iraq, where he could count on considerable support in his effort to assume the leadership of the Muslims. However, before Husayn reached Kufa, a much larger Umayyad force attacked his party at a place called Karbala. The Umayyads subjected Husayn's companions to an unrelenting volley of arrows. One by one, Husayn's supporters fell until, among the fighters, only he remained standing. Finally, the Umayyads killed Husayn in the fighting. The Umayyads took captive the surviving women and children and decapitated the bodies of the fallen fighters, leaving them unburied. The massacre took place in the year 680, on October 10—the 10th (*Ashura*, in Arabic) of the Muslim month of Muharram.

Afterward, Yazid's victorious army took Husayn's head to the Umayyad capital of Damascus and put it on display. However, Husayn's son Ali, known as Zayn al-Abdin, survived Karbala to carry on the genealogical line. The Shia consider him to have been the fourth Imam.

In the Shia perspective, Husayn is a great martyr, someone who sacrificed his life for justice and the greater good. Each year, on the 10th of Muharram, Shia communities everywhere commemorate Husayn's death in public processions of mourning

Shiites participate in an annual pilgrimage to Karbala, Iraq, home to a shrine to Imam Husayn, grandson of the Prophet Muhammad. Husayn and his supporters were massacred at Karbala in 680 C.E. This event marked the permanent division of the Islamic community into Sunni and Shia branches. Shiites commemorate Husayn's martyrdom during their holiday of Ashura.

The emotional devotion of Shia Muslims to their traditions is nowhere more evident than in their journeys to various shrines. The tombs of Imams, martyrs, and saints are considered sacred places where pilgrims receive spiritual power and comfort. Here, Shiites carry a casket during a ceremony observing the death of the seventh Imam, Musa al-Kazim.

and reenactments (*ta'ziya*) of the tragedy at Karbala. The latter usually take place in large halls called *husaniyyat* built near mosques or in town and city squares. Accompanied by poems and lamentations, actors portray Husayn and his companions and the Umayyad leaders held responsible for the massacre. For the Shia, the story of Husayn's martyrdom calls to mind the suffering that takes place in the world, and the fact that sometimes injustice and tyranny will triumph over justice and goodness. The ritual mourning for Husayn enables Shia to come to terms with this reality and dedicate themselves to God's truth. Throughout history, Shia have reviled unpopular governments by associating them with the opponents of the Imam Husayn.

The Shia venerate the tomb of Husayn at Karbala, that of Ali at Najaf, and the tombs of other subsequent Imams as shrines. Shia will attempt to visit these holy places as pilgrims and will make every effort to bring the bodies of their dead relatives for burial in their environs.

Twelver Shiism's Hidden Imam

The Shia view themselves as a righteous yet oppressed community. The themes of suffering and martyrdom are prominent in Shia religious literature and practice.

However, the Shia believe that one day justice will prevail in the world. This expectation centers on the twelfth Imam, Abu al-Qasim Muhammad. According to Shia tradition, Abu al-Qasim Muhammad disappeared in a well inside a cave at Samarra in Iraq in 874 C.E. when he was a young boy. His followers claimed that he had entered a state of hiding, or occultation, in order to gain protection from his enemies. At first, the "Hidden Imam" continued to communicate with humanity through four representatives who relayed to him messages and questions from the Shia faithful. The Shia refer to this stage of indirect communication as the Lesser Occultation. However, in 941, under the threat of the Sunnis, the Hidden Imam entered the period of Greater Occultation, which continues to the present moment. In the Greater Occultation, the twelfth Imam is still the spiritual guide. However, he is no longer in direct communication with the Shia. Rather, God has completely concealed him from the eyes of men. For the Shia, the Greater

A Shia cleric speaks to an audience of believers in the United States. Shia communities can be found in many countries around the world, although most Shiites live in the Middle East—particularly in modern-day Iraq and Iran.

Occultation is a profound spiritual tragedy for the world. It means that the spiritual guide to humanity is out of reach.

Nevertheless, the Hidden Imam will eventually leave his Greater Occultation and reappear to the world. At that time, he will take the title Mahdi, or "Guided One." This return will occur shortly before the Final Judgment and the end of history. Imam Mahdi will return at the head of an army of righteousness and do battle with the forces of evil in one final, apocalyptic battle. When evil has been defeated, Imam Mahdi will rule under a perfect government and bring about a perfect spirituality among the peoples of the world. After Imam Mahdi has reigned for several years, Jesus Christ will return, as will Husayn and others. The concept of a Mahdi who will appear before the end of time to "fill the earth with justice after it has been filled with injustice and tyranny" is common to both Sunni and Shia Islam. However, whereas the Sunnis believe that the Mahdi can be any descendant of Ali and Fatima, the Shia explicitly identify him with the twelfth Imam.

Some modern scholars believe that political reasons lay behind the twelfth Imam's disappearance. They argue that as long as the Imams were physically present in the world, the Sunni rulers regarded them as potential threats to their authority. Consequently, the Sunni authorities would closely monitor and sometimes persecute the Shia followers of the Imams, regarding them as sources of dissidence. Removing the worldly reality of the Imam was a way for community leaders to secure the economic prosperity and peaceful existence of the Shia. At the same time, the Lesser and Greater Occultations allowed the doctrine of adherence to the Imam to continue.

The Greater Occultation presented the Shia community with a grave problem. Without the guidance of the Imam who was in

The shrine of Fatima, sister of the eighth Imam, is located in Qom, Iran. Shiites consider Qom a sacred city, and hundreds of Muslim saints are buried there.

"hiding," how were the Shia to discern God's will? How should they conduct their day-to-day affairs? Furthermore, what attitude should they adopt toward the Sunni caliphs, whom they regarded as illegitimate? The Shia solution to the first issue was remarkably similar to that devised in the Sunni community, where the religious scholars (ulama) provided guidance to the Muslims in the absence of the Prophet Muhammad. In a similar fashion, Shia religious scholars became the heirs of the Imams. Of course, they could not claim the Imam's infallibility, but they could fulfill certain functions on his behalf until the return of Imam Mahdi. By the 16th century, Shia jurists determined that these functions included implementing Islamic law (Sharia), waging defensive jihad against enemies, collecting religious taxes, and leading the Friday prayer.

In comparison with their Sunni counterparts, Shia clergy are more hierarchically organized. The Shia refer to the top-ranking religious scholars as *mujtahids*. These are men who literally "strive" to understand the will of God and the guidance of the Imams through the study of the Qur'an, the Traditions of the Prophet Muhammad, and the Traditions of the Imams, as well as by applying independent reason to the Qur'an and the Traditions. In utilizing this methodology, the mujtahids interpret law and doctrine in order to deal with changing social, economic, and political conditions. Nevertheless, the mujtahids claim to achieve only probable knowledge of the Imam's intentions. Since their judgment is necessarily imperfect, the mujtahids allow differences of opinion among themselves. Yet it is necessary that each Shia follow the guidance of a living mujtahid. There might be four or five prominent mujtahids at any given time, and believers can choose which to follow. Beginning in the 20th century, the Shia came to refer to the most prominent mujtahids as "ayatollahs" (literally, "signs of God") and aspiring mujtahids as *"Hujjat al-Islam"* ("the proof of Islam"). From time

When on pilgrimage to the shrine of one of their Imams, Shiites may refer to prayer books. During prayer, a Shiite worshipper will touch his forehead to the turba, or clay disc pictured on top of this book.

to time, the mujtahids recognize one from among them to be designated as a supreme, or grand, ayatollah. Today, an example of a grand ayatollah is Ali Sistani, who hails from Iran but is settled at Najaf in Iraq.

How does a person become a mujtahid? The process is relatively informal. First, a young man must attend a religious school (*madrasa*) in a place such as Najaf or Qom in Iran, where he becomes an expert in theology, jurisprudence, science, and philosophy. After years of study, he begins delivering lectures of his own, offering unique, insightful interpretations of Islamic texts. He starts to write religious books of his own, and young students seek out his wisdom. Eventually, his fame spreads beyond Islamic academic circles. Once the scholar has gained a critical mass of followers and earned the respect of established teachers, he is generally considered a mujtahid.

As regards the issue of Shia relations with Sunni caliphs and other Sunni leaders, the Shia decided to recognize passively their political authority, while privately regarding them as illegitimate. In adopting this position, the Shia understood that the twelfth Imam (Imam Mahdi) would one day restore legitimate government. In the meantime, the Shia had no choice but to accept their subject status under Sunni rule, for bad or illegitimate government was preferable to no government at all, which would give rise to anarchy. Consequently, obedience to the ruler became a religious obligation among the Shia, even if the ruler were unjust.

However, this traditional Shia deference to political power changed in the middle decades of the 20th century. During this period, a number of religious scholars challenged the secular authority of the Shah ("king") of Iran, accusing him of corruption and misrule. One of these scholars, the Ayatollah Khomeini, wrote a book in 1971 called *The Guardianship of the Islamic*

Shia leaders like Grand Ayatollah Ali Khamenei hold both religious and political power in Shia communities. Khamenei has served as Iran's Supreme Leader since the death of Ayatollah Khomeini in 1989.

Jurist, in which he argued that the most prominent mujtahid of the time had the right to represent the Hidden Imam in his role as political leader in addition to representing him in his religious functions. The Ayatollah Khomeini's theory of the guardianship of the jurist provided the theoretical justification for the clerical rule that took hold in Iran in the 1979 Islamic Revolution. As the best-qualified mujtahid, the Ayatollah Khomeini became the first Supreme Leader of the Islamic Republic of Iran. As leader, he offered Iranians and other Shia sympathetic to his cause the expert guidance that he had written about earlier.

The Ismailis

The Twelvers constitute the largest group within Shiism. Another important Shia community is that of the Ismailis. In the Middle Ages, the Ismailis were based largely in Iran. However, sizable Ismaili communities also came to exist in India, Pakistan, Syria, East Africa, and Central Asia. During the last decades of the 20th century, Ismailis emigrated from these countries to Great Britain, Canada, Australia, New Zealand, and the United States. Altogether, there are about 15 million Ismailis in the world.

The Ismailis take their name from Ismail, elder son of the sixth Imam, Ja'far al-Sadiq. Ismail died before his father. But the Ismailis believe that before Ismail's death, Ja'far al-Sadiq had already designated him as his successor to the Imamate, and that prior to his own death Ismail in turn designated his son Muhammad. Sometimes the Ismailis are called Seveners because, in the Ismaili view, Ismail is the legitimate seventh Imam. Consequently, Ismailis follow the line of Imams from Ismail. However, the Twelvers deny this, claiming that Ja'far al-Sadiq

This page from a rare ninth-century copy of the Qur'an features gold ink on colored vellum. This ornate edition of the Qur'an was produced in Tunisia, where the Ismaili sect thrived during the eighth and ninth centuries.

passed over Ismail for the succession because he predeceased his father. For the Twelvers, the seventh Imam is Ja'far's second son, Musa al-Kazim. The Abbasid caliph Harun al-Rashid poisoned Musa in 799.

During the late eighth and early ninth centuries, Muhammad and his son organized the intricate hierarchical structure and propaganda machine of the sect. Over the following two centuries, as the Abbasid caliphate entered into turmoil, Ismailism inspired revolutionary movements throughout the Middle East and North Africa. Ismailism was especially popular among oppressed peasants, slaves, and townspeople.

The Ismailis organized themselves into a hierarchical secret society. The leader of a particular region was called the *da'i*, or chief "missionary." Following the Shia practice of taqiyya (hiding one's true beliefs), the Ismaili movement was kept secret.

Da'is forbade members to reveal anything about the doctrines or makeup of the community. The Ismaili Imam sent da'is to all parts of the Muslim world with the object of setting up Ismaili cells everywhere. In the 10th century the Ismailis sent missionaries to North Africa. They succeeded in converting the Kutama Berbers of Ifriqiya (present-day Tunisia) to their faith. The Berbers resented the control of the Sunni Abbasids over them and were therefore quick to accept the revolutionary Ismaili ideology. In 908, with the ground prepared by his missionaries, the Ismaili Imam Ubayd Allah al-Mahdi—who had been living in Salamiyya, Syria—declared himself the first Fatimid caliph in Ifriqiya. (The name Fatimid derived from the Ismaili Imams' descent from Ali and the Prophet's daughter Fatima.)

The first three Fatimid caliphs ruled only in Ifriqiya. In 969 Imam Mu'izz, the fourth Fatimid caliph, conquered Egypt. He

Continued on page 38

A modern view of al-Azhar University in Cairo, Egypt, which was founded in the 10th century by a Fatimid caliph. At one time al-Azhar was the center of Ismaili scholarship and religious thought. Today it is the most highly respected university in the Sunni Muslim world.

What Ismailis Believe

Ismaili doctrine distinguishes between the literal teaching of the Qur'an and the mystical truth hidden behind it. Every verse of the Qur'an has a literal (*Zahir*) and a hidden (*Batin*) meaning that is discerned by those trained in the use of allegory, symbolism, and numerology. Spiritual guides reveal these hidden truths to initiates in carefully programmed stages. The inner meanings often contradict the plain meanings of the Qur'anic passage. In the Ismaili system, an individual's salvation depends on his recognizing this secret knowledge.

The Ismaili disciple is thus made aware of the "divine secrets" of the universe. By oath, he is also bound to recognize the spiritual hierarchy of the sect (headed by the Imam), which operates as a secret society. In the 10th century, a group of Ismaili scholars in Basra, Iraq, formed a secret society called "The Brethren of Purity." They wrote a philosophical encyclopedia, "The Epistles of the Brethren of Purity" (*Rasa'il Ikhwan al-Safa*). It endeavored to include all the human knowledge of that time. The Brethren of Purity believed all religions to be an outward manifestation of the spiritual truths they had discovered. Their epistles were popular in all Muslim lands from India to Spain and strongly influenced later Muslim thinkers.

Ismailis emphasize the unity of God. In keeping with this belief, they avoid describing God as having human attributes (such as hands or a face, or as sitting on a throne). In their view, God is transcendent and unknowable. Because God is beyond human understanding, there must be intermediaries between him and our material world. These take the form of a hierarchy of emanations—lesser Gods who separated from the Divine Essence. The first emanation is the Universal Intellect. From the Universal Intellect emanates the Universal Soul, from which proceed the mineral, animal, and vegetable orders of the physical world. Through spiritual and intellectual effort, the Ismailis seek to attain knowledge of the Universal Soul and the Divine Essence behind it.

One of the most interesting aspects of Ismaili thought is the idea of cyclical time. According to the Ismailis, history goes through a cycle of seven eras. Each cycle is started by a Speaker Prophet (a legislating prophet, or messenger), who brings a scripture with a law. The Speaker Prophet is accompanied by a Silent One, who understands the hidden truth concealed in the scripture. Thus, Moses had Aaron, Jesus had Peter, and Muhammad had Ali. Because of his interpretive function, the Silent One is of more importance than the Speaker Prophet, who communicates the divine message but does not expound on its true meaning. The Silent One is followed by a series of seven Imams. The seventh Imam assumes the rank of Speaker of the next cycle. The last Imam, when he appears, will do away with all organized religions and their laws and will bring about a new era with a universal religion. Upon the conclusion of that cycle, God will end the world.

Although Ismailism often had a popular following, its religious doctrines appealed mostly to Muslim intellectuals. Ismaili philosophers and scientists were some of the most innovative and sophisticated thinkers of the Muslim Middle Ages. An Ismaili convert, Nasir al-Din Tusi (1201–1274), for example, proposed a new model of planetary motion. For the Ismailis, science was a meditation of God's creation, a way of understanding rationally the assumptions accepted as part of revelation. Currently, the Institute of Ismaili Studies in London, England, is sponsoring research on the Ismaili scholarly heritage.

established Cairo as his capital and founded the mosque-university of al-Azhar as the religious center of Ismailism. The Fatimids ruled Egypt for two centuries, during which time they competed with the Abbasids for control of the Muslim world. They rapidly expanded their empire into Syria, Palestine, and Arabia, including Mecca and Medina. The Ismailis viewed the Fatimid caliph as the infallible Imam who held both religious and secular authority.

In 1094 al-Afdal, the *wazir* (chief minister), assassinated Nizar, heir to the caliphate, and appointed Nizar's younger brother, al-Musta'li, as caliph. This created a split in Ismailism between those who remained faithful to Nizar and his line and

Prince Karim Aga Khan IV has served as the hereditary Imam of the Ismailis since 1957. He has worked to improve the quality of life within Ismaili communities around the world. Over the years the Aga Khan has also given generously to social and economic development projects in Third World countries of Africa and Asia.

those who accepted Musta'li. Nizar's supporters (called "Nizaris") established themselves in Syria and Iran, where they engaged in a campaign of assassination against the Sunni leaders of the Seljuk sultanate. For some reason, some refer to the Nizaris as "The Assassins." The Musta'lis, on the other hand, continued in Egypt and had a base of support in Yemen. The Sunni sultan Saladin abolished the Egypt-based Fatimid caliphate in 1171. Saladin and his successors transformed al-Azhar into a Sunni mosque. Following Saladin's conquest, Ismailism in Egypt slowly disappeared. However, the supporters of Nizar continued to exist and flourish in the mountains of Syria and Iran. They dispersed after the Mongol invasion of the 13th century. In the 19th century, the Iranian Shah bestowed the title "Aga Khan" upon the Nizari line of Ismaili Imams. The current holder of the title, Prince Karim Aga Khan IV, is the 49th Ismaili Imam, tracing his lineage back to Ali, cousin of the Prophet Muhammad.

Other Shia Subgroups

Shiism is itself fragmented in a way not found in Sunni Islam. As in the Ismaili case, the dominant divisions have to do with the nature of the Imamate and with questions of succession. Three Shia or Shia-derived groups deserve mention because they illustrate some of the directions Shiism has taken, in addition to being interesting in their own right. These three are the Zaydis, the Nusayris (or Alawis), and the Druze.

Zaydis

Zaydis disagree with Twelvers and Ismailis over the identity of the fifth Imam. Twelvers and Ismailis recognize Imam Husayn's grandson, Muhammad al-Baqir (died ca. 731) as the rightful Imam. A minority followed al-Baqir's brother, Zayd (d. 740). For this reason, Zayd's followers are known as Zaydis. Outsiders sometimes refer to them as "Fivers."

Pedestrians walk through the gate to the old section of Sana'a, the capital of Yemen. Most of the world's Zaydi Muslims live in this country on the Arabian Peninsula.

Zayd was the first person after the massacre of Husayn and his family to try to wrest political power from the Umayyads. After spending a year in preparation in the heavily Shia city of Kufa in Iraq, he and his followers challenged the caliph Hashim. However, Zayd's forces were defeated and he was killed in battle.

Zaydi beliefs are somewhat similar to those of the largest Shia sect, the Twelvers. The major difference is that Zaydis believe that any male descendant of Ali and Fatima can be Imam regardless of whether he descends from Husayn or from his elder brother Hasan. In order to assume the title Imam, a person must have the will and ability to resort to force against the community's enemies if necessary. He must also possess high moral character and religious learning. Thus, whereas Zayd displayed moral rectitude in fighting against corrupt rulers, his brother, Muhammad al-Baqir, did not show such qualities and was therefore an unsuitable candidate for the Imamate. If a candidate for the Imamate does not live up to all these requirements, the Zaydis will not recognize him as a full Imam. Rather, they will regard him as an inferior Imam of either martial skill or learning only. The Zaydis do not believe in the infallibility of the Imams, or that the Imams receive divine guidance. Nor do they believe in the possibility of a hidden Imam who is not present in the world to carry out his functions. The observance of taqiyya (hiding one's true beliefs) is also alien to Zaydi belief. Because of the high standards required of a Zaydi Imam, it is possible that there might be an age without an Imam.

Zaydi Shiism never gained a great following and in modern times is almost entirely limited to the rugged mountains of northern Yemen. The Zaydi presence in Yemen goes back to the late ninth century. About 40 percent of the country's population adheres to this form of Shiism. Today, the Zaydis are believed to number up to 9.5 million.

Nusayris (Alawis)

Nusayrism has affinities with Shiism, especially Ismaili Shiism. However, because Nusayris incorporate into their faith certain doctrines that go against the basic teachings of Islam, Muslims generally regard them as outside of Islam. Almost all Nusayris live in Syria, where they are concentrated in the mountainous Latakiyya region. A small number of Nusayris live in southeastern Turkey. Altogether, the Nusayris number around 700,000.

Nusayris take their name from Muhammad Bin Nusayr, who was a disciple of Ali al-Hadi (d. 868) and Hasan al-Askari

Syrian president Bashar al-Asad is perhaps the highest-profile member of the Nusayri (or Alawite) sect of Islam. Approximately 70 percent of Syrians adhere to the mainstream Sunni branch of the faith. However, the Nusayri, who make up perhaps 15 to 20 percent of Syria's population, have a strong influence on the country's government.

(d. 873), the tenth and eleventh Imams, respectively. However, in modern times Nusayris tend to call themselves Alawis to underscore their link with Ali ibn Abi Talib, the common ancestor of all Shia factions. In the 20th century, Nusayris have enjoyed a degree of political dominance that is disproportionate to their size. After the First World War the French, who were ruling Syria at the time, encouraged the Nusayris to join Syria's armed forces. Since 1970, following the coup of the Nusayri air force chief, Hafiz al-Asad, the Nusayris have been dominant in Syrian political and military life.

Nusayris have their own distinct religious leaders, called shaykhs. Nusayris believe that these shaykhs have a kind of divine authority. One of the shaykh's duties is to lead religious and other ceremonies during which Nusayris celebrate their sacred figures. At the age of 19, Nusayris undergo an initiation rite in which they begin to learn some of the secrets of the sect. The initiation ceremony confirms membership in the Nusayri community.

Mystery shrouds Nusayri religious beliefs. In fact, only initiates know the details of the Nusayri creed. Nevertheless, it is apparent that their beliefs are similar in broad outline to Ismaili Shiism. Like the Ismailis, the Nusayris believe in emanations that spring from a transcendent God. One of these emanations is the Name (*ism*). The other is the Gate (*bab*). God reveals these emanations in seven historical periods. In each period, the emanations take the form of historical persons. During the seventh and last cycle, called the Muhammadan cycle, the emanations have been incarnated by Ali (the Divine Essence), Muhammad (the Name), and Salman al-Farsi, an early Persian convert to Islam (the Gate).

The Nusayris observe a number of religious festivals, not all of them Islamic in inspiration. Thus, they recognize Easter,

Epiphany, the Persian New Year (Nawruz), the 10th of Muharram, and the Muslim feasts of Eid al-Fitr and Eid al-Adha.

Druze

The Druze religion has its roots in Ismailism. Most Muslims do not consider the Druze as adherents of Islam because they regard the Fatimid caliph Al-Hakim bi-Amr Allah, the sixth Fatimid caliph of Egypt, as a manifestation of God. The Druze believe that God hid him away and that he will return as the Mahdi on Judgment Day. Like Nusayris, most Druze keep the tenets of their faith secret. Druze origins date to the 11th century, when a Persian Ismaili preacher named Hamza propagated the seeds of what became the Druze doctrine. Hamza's successor, al-Darazi (from which the name "Druze" is derived), further developed the message among the mountain-dwelling populations of southern Lebanon and Syria. Active proselytizing of the new creed was brief. Since al-Darazi's time, the Druze have closed their community to outsiders. In modern times, small communities of Druze spread in Europe, North America, and South America. During the British Mandate over Palestine, the Druze refrained from taking part in the Arab-Jewish conflict. However, during the first Arab-Israeli war (1948–49), the community actively supported Israel. The majority of Druze live in Syria, Lebanon, Israel, and Jordan.

The Druze are divided into two classes of people. Most Druze, called al-Juhal ("the Ignorant"), do not have access to Druze holy literature, although they practice personal prayer. The religious elite, which includes both men and women, is called al-Uqqal ("the Knowledgeable Initiates"). It comprises about 20 percent of the total Druze population. The Uqqal wear special dress in compliance with Qur'anic norms. Women wear a white headscarf, especially in the presence of other people, and black shirts and long skirts. Male Uqqal grow mustaches, have shaven heads, and wear dark clothing with white turbans. The community chooses from among the elite the Shaykh al-Aql, who functions as the political, social, and religious leader of the Druze.

Like the Ismailis and the Shia subgroups, the Druze uphold the strict and uncompromising unity of God. God does not have attributes. At the same time, he is present in the world. The Druze also believe that the teachings of the prophets and religious scriptures have both obvious and hidden meanings; the former are apparent only to a select few within the religious elite. The Druze religion has few ceremonies and rituals, and no obligation to perform precepts in public. The main tenets that obligate all Druze, both Uqqal and Juhal, are: 1) Speaking the truth; 2) Supporting your brethren; 3) Abandoning the old creeds; 4) Purification from heresy; 5) Accepting the unity of God; and 6) Submitting to the will of God.

Members of a Druze community in Palestine, circa 1900. Today, most of the Druze live in Israel, Lebanon, Syria, and Jordan.

Sufism

Sufism is the mystical dimension of Islam. Sufism is not technically a division within Islam, such as the Shia. Rather, Sufism is an expression of Islam. Sufis, like mystics in other religious traditions, are not satisfied with the formal practice of religion. The Sufi aims in his or her devotions to experience God first hand. Although Sufism is widespread throughout the Islamic world, puritanical Muslims tend to denounce Sufism on two counts. First, they say, Sufism introduces into Islam practices and beliefs that are not in keeping with the tenets of the faith. Second, they accuse the Sufis of collapsing the radical distinction between God and his creation in their effort to establish communion with God.

Despite the tension between doctrinal Islam and Sufi practices, each side accepted the other as necessary. Because Sufism attracted mass conversions to Islam, the ulama tolerated a variety of Sufi rituals. For their part, the Sufis were not opposed to the doctrinaire Islam of the ulama but saw the need for the kind of emotive dimension of the Islamic experience that Sufism offered.

As the Sharia bound society together under a uniform legal system, the Sufi brotherhoods functioned as a structured subsystem in which people's mystical inclinations found an outlet.

The origins of Sufism lie in a very informal movement of personal piety that emerged in the first century of Islam. These earliest Sufis emphasized prayer, asceticism, and withdrawal from society. The term *Sufism*—or *tasawwuf*, as the tradition is called in Arabic—may derive from the practice of wearing wool (*suf* in Arabic), or possibly from the Arabic word for purity (*safa*). The earliest Sufis spent almost all of their waking hours in prayer, and they frequently engaged in acts of spiritual self-discipline, such as starving themselves and denying themselves sleep. They renounced their connections to the world and possessed little apart from the clothes on their backs. A number of the early Sufis were women, several of whom, such as Rabia al-Adawiyya (717–801), are revered to this day.

It is very likely that the Sufis adopted the practices of asceticism and the wearing of wool after observing the Christian ascetics of Syria and Palestine. Sufis, however, see the origins of their movement in the Qur'an and the life of Muhammad. They are quick to observe that Muhammad lived an extremely simple, almost ascetic, life, and that he had a habit of withdrawing from Mecca to meditate in a cave. Indeed, it was while he was meditating in this manner that Muslims believe he received his first revelation. Sufis therefore see their practices as an imitation of Muhammad, and they hope to achieve the same close relationship with God as he enjoyed.

According to Islamic belief, all Muslims will have a direct encounter with God after they die (opinions differ as to what this means), but Sufis do not wish to wait that long. Sufis consider the direct encounter with God so overwhelming as to be expressible only in metaphors. The most commonly used metaphors are those

This shrine to a Sufi shaykh known as Rukn-e-Alam ("Pillar of the World") is located in Multan, Pakistan. Today, many Muslims in South Asia observe the mystical teachings and practices of Sufism.

of falling in love and of being intoxicated with wine. Sufis often refer to the union with God as *fana*, which literally means destruction or annihilation. Sufis believe that in the final stage of an individual's spiritual development, he or she loses any consciousness of individual identity and is only aware of the identity of God. In effect, God's identity then replaces the identity of the Sufi.

Sufis disagree about whether the final spiritual goal of Sufism is to lose one's identity completely in the identity of God, or to reach a stage where one's own petty concerns no longer prevent one from seeing the world in its true nature. A common metaphor for the first approach is to describe the Sufi's individuality as a drop, which vanishes into the ocean. It does not actually cease to exist, for it is now part of the vastness of the sea. It only ceases to exist insofar as it is an individual drop. The latter view depicts the human heart (considered the seat of the intellect in medieval Islamic thought) as a mirror that is normally dirty, tarnished by everyday concerns and petty desires. Through engaging in mystical exercises Sufis effectively polish the mirror of the heart to the point where it can accurately reflect the light of God.

For Sufis, the quest for spiritual understanding is a path that they must travel under the guidance of a teacher or master. This path has many stages, the number and names of which vary depending on the school of Sufi thought. In most instances, the first stage on the Sufi path is one of repentance. The Sufi repents of all his or her bad deeds and takes a vow to avoid all earthly pleasures. Often the Sufi is then required to divest himself or herself of earthly belongings, which may include attachments to friends and family. After having done these things, Sufis traditionally enter a monastery and devote themselves fully to the difficult task of shedding earthly concerns. In practice, this process of divestment is extremely difficult, often takes a long time, and requires strict, spiritual direction under a master.

Sufis rely on meditation to accomplish their goals. Sufis refer to the various forms of meditation as *dhikr*. Dhikr literally means remembrance; in the Qur'an it appears in the context of urging Muslims to remember God frequently. At its most basic level, Sufi dhikr consists of repeating one of God's names. In Islam, God has 99 names that represent his character and qualities. These include *Rahim* (merciful), *Wahid* (unique), and *Hayy* (Living). The purpose of reciting these names is to concentrate wholly on what one is doing and to lose all self-awareness. One's entire being identifies with the dhikr formula through repetition, so that even if one ceases actively to engage in dhikr, one continues to repeat it in one's heart. Some dhikr exercises involve the repetition of longer formulas, while others also entail complicated methods of breath control. Dhikrs are sometimes supplemented with music and dance called *sama*, which are aimed at bringing the Sufi to a state of spiritual ecstasy.

The Sufi Orders

The development of Sufism followed a general pattern: Groups of devotees would gather around a local religious figure whose stature rested on his ability to commune with God by means of a particular dhikr. In the 12th and 13th centuries, groups of Sufis who practiced the same ritual and followed the same master formed themselves into structured brotherhoods called *tariqas*. The Sufi "chain" (*silsila*) of authority, which traced the dhikr back to the master, guaranteed the soundness of the teaching. The Sufi master and his successors (normally called "caliphs"— not to be confused with the political leaders of the Islamic world in medieval times) would invest his disciples with a patched garment (*khirqa*) as a sign of their joining the brotherhood. Although most brotherhood organizations were local, several established regional branches, and a few managed to set up networks throughout the world of Islam. In many places, the brotherhoods set up lodges (called in Persian *khanqahs*; in Arabic, *zawiyas*), which provided services to the community, such as distributing food to the poor, organizing relief in times of famine or illness, and in general serving as a focal point of social as well as religious life. Until the onset of the modern period in the 19th and 20th centuries, a majority of Muslims found spiritual fulfillment in the Sufi experience.

Many Sufi orders have been important in the evolution of Islamic society. Three orders deserve special attention: the Chisti, the Mawlawis, and the Naqshbandis.

The Chisti order takes its name from Khaja Mu'in al-Din Chisti (d. 1235), who came from a town in Afghanistan and settled in the city of Ajmer in India. There he taught a large number of influential disciples. The brotherhood that he founded included many converts from Hinduism, especially from the lower castes, who were attracted to its egalitarian message. These disciples opened Chisti centers in provincial towns all over India. At the same time, the order attracted many Indian rulers. It rapidly became the most influential order in the Indian Subcontinent. The Chisti order has as its dhikr a particular kind of musical performance called *qawwali*, in which a group of musicians sing religious songs, composed in regional languages, set to a rhythmic beat. The Pakistani singer Nusrat Fateh Ali Khan (1948–1997), whose music became popular in Europe and North America, was the best-known modern exponent of the qawwali. Although the Chisti brotherhood became the most important Sufi order in India, it never spread beyond the Indian Subcontinent.

The Mawlawi order was largely limited to Turkish Anatolia (modern-day Turkey) during the Seljuk and Ottoman periods (13th to the early 20th centuries), although it had some influence in Arabic-speaking countries such as Egypt. The order derives its name from the famous Persian mystical poet Jalal al-Din Rumi (1207–1273), called Mevlana in Turkish. Rumi was born in Central Asia. The Mongol invasion of that region forced the family to move to Konya, the seat of the Seljuk sultans, in Anatolia. In 1244, Rumi fell under the spell of a wandering mystic named Shams-e Tabrizi. Shams mysteriously disappeared, but Rumi continued on the spiritual path. He devoted himself to writing mystical poetry. He also began to attract disciples whom he provided with spiritual guidance. Thus was founded the Mawlawi Sufi order.

Music and dance distinguish the Mawlawi dhikr. Typically, the Mawlawis recite prayers and hymns after which they dance in a whirling motion with arms outstretched. One hand faces upward to receive God's grace, and the other hand faces downward to dispense the grace to humanity. For good reason, the Mawlawi order is known in the West as the "Whirling Dervishes" (the word *dervish* means something like "poor mendicant"—someone who lives an ascetic lifestyle, going door to door asking for food). In the 20th century, the secular Turkish government severely restricted the activities of the Mawlawi and

The *Masnavi-I Ma'navi*, written by the influential mystic poet Rumi (1207–1273), is considered one of the most important works of Sufi literature. In six volumes, Rumi presents poems that illustrate the Muslim's search for Allah. This manuscript, which dates from 1278, is on display at Rumi's tomb in Konya, Turkey.

The so-called Whirling Dervishes of the Turkish Mawlawi Sufi order perform their traditional dance.

other Sufi orders, fearing their abilities to spread "emotionalism" and "superstition" among the masses.

Unlike the Chisti and Mawlawi Sufi orders, which are both ethnically and geographically limited in range, the Naqshbandi brotherhood is more widely distributed, with branches throughout the Islamic world. The brotherhood is named after a Central Asian Sufi, a Tajik from Bukhara named Baha al-Din Naqshaband (d. 1389). One of the brotherhood's most distinctive features is the "silent dhikr," spoken through the heart, which Naqshbandis practice alongside a conventional spoken dhikr. Naqshbandis believe that Sufis should express their piety through social activity rather than withdrawal from society. This activist orientation encouraged the Naqshbandis to cooperate with political powers when necessary, but to resist them by force when circumstances made this desirable.

Naqshbandi figures were very important in religious reform movements in the 18th and 19th centuries, especially in India and Central Asia, where Muslims were fighting British and Russian colonialism, respectively. In India, the Naqshbandi shaykh Shah Wali Allah led the push for a more rigorous application of the Sharia in society. In the 19th and 20th centuries, a wide range of Naqshbandi groups encouraged the Turkish-speaking subject peoples of the czarist Russian Empire and the Soviet Union to resist Russian domination.

Chronology

632: On March 10, at a place called Ghadir Khumm, the Prophet Muhammad shares a Qur'anic revelation that the Shia interpret as appointing Ali ibn Abi Talib as his successor. After Muhammad's death, however, Abu Bakr assumes the leadership of the Islamic community, accepting the name of caliph ("successor of the Prophet") on June 8.

644: Umar, the second caliph, dies and is succeeded by Uthman, a member of the Umayyad family.

656: The third caliph, Uthman, is murdered, and Ali becomes the new caliph.

657: Ali and Mu'awiyya agree to negotiate their differences over the fate of Uthman's murderers at Siffin on the Euphrates River. During the negotiations, the Kharijites leave Ali's camp.

661: A Kharijite murders Ali as he prays at the mosque in Najaf. Mu'awiyya becomes caliph and founds the Umayyad dynasty.

680: Husayn, second son of Ali, challenges Umayyad rule and is killed at Karbala during the reign of the caliph Yazid.

740: Revolt of Zayd, recognized as the fifth Imam by his followers, who are known as Zaydis.

750: The Abbasid family overthrows the Umayyad dynasty. Among the supporters of the Abbasids are many Shia.

799: Musa al-Kazim, recognized by the Ismailis as the seventh Imam, dies.

874: The Lesser Occultation of Abu al-Qasim Muhammad, the twelfth Imam, begins.

941: The Greater Occultation of the twelfth Imam begins; Twelver Shiites believe it continues to the present day.

Glossary

Aga Khan—a title granted by the Shah of Persia to the Ismaili Imam in 1818 and inherited by each of his successors to the Imamate.

ayatollah—a title (literally, "Sign of God") for a religious leader of the Twelver Shia. The ayatollah usually heads the hierarchy among the Twelver Shia mujtahids and is considered a primary source for religious learning.

caliph—the head of the Muslim community in Sunni Islam.

dhikr—remembrance for the sake of Allah. Dhikr designates a kind of prayer, which consists in the constant repetition of a name or formula. It is performed either in solitude or collectively.

Fatimids—a Muslim dynasty of Ismailis based in Egypt (973–1171), who claimed descent from the Prophet Muhammad through Ali. They derived their name from the Prophet's daughter, Fatima.

Ibadis—adherents of a branch of the Kharijites, named after their seventh-century leader Abdullah ibn Ibad.

Imam—in general usage, an Islamic leader of prayers or religious leader. The Shia use the term for their spiritual leaders descended from Ali ibn Abi Talib and the Prophet Muhammad's daughter Fatima.

Ismailis—adherents of a branch of Shia Islam that considers Ismail, the eldest son of Imam Ja'far al-Sadiq, as his successor.

jihad—used in Muslim writing to denote "the struggle." Muslims distinguish between the Greater Jihad, which is the struggle to become a better Muslim, and the Lesser Jihad, which is the endeavor to spread Islam in the world and defend it from enemies.

Kharijites—a group of early Muslims who withdrew their allegiance from Ali.

Mahdi—the "rightly guided one," a name applied to the restorer of true religion and justice expected at the end of time. In Twelver Shiism the word *Mahdi* refers specifically to the hidden Imam.

mujtahid—in Twelver Shiism, high-ranking religious scholars who formulate their own religious and judicial principles.

Sharia—the standard term used for Muslim law; the totality of the Islamic way of life.

shaykh—an old man, elder, or tribal chief. Often used as an honorific title for any religious dignitary, in particular a Sufi master or spiritual guide.

Twelvers—the majority branch of the Shia Muslims who acknowledge twelve Imams in succession from Ali after the Prophet Muhammad. Following Imam Ja'far al-Sadiq, the Twelvers acknowledged his younger son Musa al-Kazim as their Imam while the Ismailis recognized Ismail, the eldest son of Imam Ja'far al-Sadiq, as their Imam.

Zaydis—the third major branch of Shia Islam, after the Twelvers and the Ismailis. The Zaydis are named after Imam Zayd, a grandson of Imam Husayn and brother of Imam Muhammad al-Baqir.

Further Reading

Chittick, William C. *Sufism: A Beginners Guide.* London: Oneworld Publications, 2007.

Momen, Moojan. *An Introduction to Shi'i Islam: The History of Twelver Shi'ism.* New Haven, Conn., and London: Yale University Press, 1985.

Moosa, Matti. *Extremist Shiites: The Ghulat Sects.* Syracuse, N.Y.: Syracuse University Press, 1985.

Ruthven, Malise. *Islam in the World.* 3rd edition. Oxford: Oxford University Press, 2006.

Schimmel, Annemarie. *Mystical Dimensions of Islam.* Chapel Hill: The University of North Carolina Press, 1978.

Waines, David. *An Introduction to Islam.* Cambridge: Cambridge University Press, 1995.

Internet Resources

http://www.iis.ac.uk/home.asp?l=en.

This Web site, from the Institute of Ismaili Studies in London, provides information about the worldwide Ismaili community and about current research on Ismaili Islam.

http://www.sistani.org/

The official Web site of Grand Ayatollah Ali al-Sistani includes an archive of Ayatollah Sistani's legal opinions.

http://www.al-islam.org/encyclopedia/list.html

This site, *A Shi'ite Encyclopedia*, provides a listing of basic beliefs of Twelver Shiism.

http://www.naqshbandi.org/

The official site of the Naqshbandi-Haqqani Sufi Order of America.

http://www.hayatidede.org/

The Mevlevi Order of America, dedicated to sharing the teachings of Jalal al-Din Rumi, the Persian mystic-poet.

http://www.balagh.net/english/shia/shia/10.htm#00011

A brief history of the twelve Imams by one of Shia Islam's most respected scholars, Allameh Tabatabaei.

Index

Numbers in **bold italics** refer to captions.